STUDIES

IN

JAPANESE "KAKKÉ,"

OR

BERIBERI.

BY

WALLACE TAYLOR, M.D.

OSAKA, 1886.

In the interest of creating a more extensive selection of rare historical book reprints, we have chosen to reproduce this title even though it may possibly have occasional imperfections such as missing and blurred pages, missing text, poor pictures, markings, dark backgrounds and other reproduction issues beyond our control. Because this work is culturally important, we have made it available as a part of our commitment to protecting, preserving and promoting the world's literature. Thank you for your understanding.

STUDIES IN JAPANESE "KAKKÉ," OR BERIBERI.

It is not my purpose to present a full treatise on kakké, but only to give those features of the disease to which I have devoted special study, and thus fill up some of the defects of English literature on this subject.

I.—HISTORY.

I confine myself to the history of this disease as found in Japanese literature. Japanese medical literature (excepting recent) was drawn from the Chinese, hence the history of kakké in Japanese embraces the history of this disease in China.

1.—CHINESE.*

The term "kakké," signifying condition of the legs (or disease of the legs), is found in ancient Chinese medical literature, and was applied to a disease corresponding to what is now known as kakké in Japan, probably as early as A.D. 300. This term is also found in medical literature of an earlier date, but the best critics consider that while the description of the disease given in these earlier works is genuine, the term "kakké" was subsequently added. The description of a disease identical in many respects with Japanese kakké is found in works of even an earlier date, but no name is given to the disease. Though this ancient literature is somewhat obscure, there is evidence to justify the opinion that a disease corresponding to Japanese kakké existed in China as early as 125 to 200 B.C.

*For much that appears under the head of "History," I am indebted to a series of articles that appeared in the "Tōkeizasshi" for 1882, by Mr. Kambe Bunya.

At least as early as A.D. 300, this disease was quite accurately described under the term "kakké."

The earlier classifications of this disease most probably included diseases having somewhat similar symptoms, such as oedema of the legs from other causes, general anasarca, ascites, paralysis of the extremities, &c.

Some of these ancient sages considered kakké a "kaze no doku," the result of a wind poison, while others attributed it to a "doku" (poison) that came up from the paddy fields, affecting first the feet and legs and then mounting higher in the body. We shall see in the future that some of these sages guessed more wisely than they knew.

The accounts given of this disease state that it appeared in the provence of Tsin, during the Tsin dynasty, which existed from 267 to 317 A.D.; and that from thence it gradually spread over the country to the east and south of the river. The ancient province of Tsin included the southern half of Shansi and the north-west portion of Honan provinces. It would appear then that "kakké" was first known in this section of China, and gradually spread over the alluvial plain east along the Hoang Ho river, and then gradually became disseminated over a large portion of the country. But spreading over the country may mean no more than that this disease was then first recognized. In the crude state of medical knowledge of that time, the disease may have prevailed ages before unrecognized. Recent Chinese medical literature is silent in regard to this disease, hence it has been thought to have disappeared from the country. European physicians practicing in China have failed to recognize this disease till recently. Within the last two years Drs. Lambeth and Park of Tsuchow, and Dr. Boone of Shanghai have met a number of cases. These gentlemen are of the opinion that there are many cases of beriberi among the Chinese. The disease has also been recognized at Fatshan, near Canton, and among the Chinese in the Hongkong city hospital. I am not aware that any European physician has yet recognized this disease in the valley of the Hoang Ho. My acquaintance with this disease in Japan would lead me to infer that beriberi would be found prevailing over a large portion of China. And when the existence of this disease in China is once recognized, a more careful examination of the cases of muscular paralysis and oedema will, I venture to predict, show many of them to be cases of beriberi. The reasons why this disease has not been sooner and more generally recognized by Europeans practicing in that country, is to be found in this : (a) that patients crowd the cliniques in such great numbers that a careful examination of each case is rendered impossible ; (b) lack of familiarity with the thought and mode of expression of the people; and (c) the imperfect description of the disease generally found in medical literature, which prevents those who have not had some experience with the disease from readily diagnosing it.

2.—Japanese.

The earliest account of this disease in Japan is found in the political history of the country. As early as A.D. 809, the historical collections of "*Nihon Kooki*" record a letter of resignation of an officer to his superior in Kiyoto, assigning as the reason of his resignation that every year he suffered from "*Ashi ke yamai*" (disease of the legs) and was therefore unable to perform the duties of his office. The earliest account of this disease in Japanese medical literature dates back to about A.D. 880. Most of the earlier medical writers drew their descriptions of this disease largely from Chinese medical works, but state that the disease was found in Japan. But little, however, appears in these earlier medical works in regard to kakké, and the reason assigned is that the infrequent reference to it in Chinese works left Japanese doctors in comparative ignorance on the subject, and they were not yet ready for original medical work. The earliest account of this disease in Japanese medical literature, bearing evidence of originality, dates back about 165 years. Since that date the references to this disease become more and more frequent, and show a better understanding of the nature of the disease. It is evident, however, that kakké was shrouded in obscurity to the most observing and inquiring Japanese doctor, and that it was no less an enigma to his mind than to the European physicians who have met this disease.

There is no history going to show where or when this disease first appeared in Japan. The earliest accounts, however, state that it was confined chiefly to Kiyoto and Yeddo, and was but little known in other localities. But this statement must be received with considerable allowance ; one reason assigned for it is that in these cities were assembled the best doctors and the greatest number of soldiers. One of the most interesting accounts of this disease, dating back 140 years, locates this mysterious disease along the Inland Sea and in Kiushiu. But wherever kakké may have originated in Japan, there is evidence conclusive to show, that within recent years it has been gradually extending to districts where it had hitherto been unknown. Being of telluric origin, it follows the analogy of malarial diseases ; the spores of the fungus which produce kakké become transported and take root in new localities, and thus the limits of this disease are being gradually extended.

II.—Anaemia and Leucocythemia.

The statements made in regard to the condition of the blood in beriberi have been contradictory. Most authors state that anaemia is one of the causes of this disease, or if not a predisposing cause, an essential accompanying element, and also that there is an increase in the number of white corpuscles in the blood. Dr. Simmons was the first to contradict this prevailing opinion. The peculiar pallor which most generally accompanies this disease has undoubtedly led to this opinion. But this appearance is deceptive ; it is not due to an impoverished condition of the blood, but to other causes. Clinical experience had led me several years ago to the conclusion that anaemia was not a predisposing cause, and if found complicating cases of kakké its association was accidental ; and to fully settle the question for myself I began a series of observations[*] on the blood of kakké patients. In the follownig tables are given the results of my investigations in this line.

---

[*] The result of these observations have been published in full in the "*Tokeizasshi*," 1883, Osaka, and in the "*Tokei Medical Journal*," 1884.

TABLE I.—ENUMERATION OF BLOOD CORPUSCLES.

Number, in order of corpuscular richness.	Sex. Male or Female.	Variety. Dry or Wet.	Number of days since kakké symptoms developed.	Number of days since previous enumeration.	Number of red corpuscles per cubic millimetre.		Per cent. of corpuscular richness.
					First enumeration.	Subsequent enumeration.	
1	m.	d.	26	...	3,815,000	...	77
2	m.	d.	72	...	3,969,000	...	79
3	m.	d.	30	...	4,204,000	...	84
4	f.	d.	35	...	4,487,000	...	89
5	f.	d.	10	...	4,706,000	...	94
6	m.	w.	25	...	5,062,000	...	101
7	m.	d.	89	...	5,636,000	...	112
8	m.	w.	72	...	5,692,000	...	113
				10	...	4,947,000	99
9	m.	d.	15	...	5,766,000	...	115
10	m.	d.	25	...	5,844,000	...	116
11	m.	d.	22	...	5,946,000	...	118
				11	...	5,714,000	114
Average					4,950,000	...	99

TABLE II.—ENUMERATION OF BLOOD CORPUSCLES.

Number, in order of corpuscular richness.	Sex, Male or Female.	Variety. Dry or Wet.	Number of days since kakké symptoms developed.	Number of days since previous enumeration.	Number of red corpuscles per cubic millimetre.		Per cent. of corpuscular richness.	Number of red corpuscles to one white
					First enumeration.	Subsequent enumeration.		
1	m.	w.	8	...	3,326,000	...	67	348
2	m.	d.	7	...	4,117,000	...	82	435
3	m.	d.	5	...	4,193,000	...	83	297
4	f.	d.	13	...	4,345,000	...	87	1545
5	m.	d.	42	...	4,357,000	...	87	720
				43	...	5,439,000	109	919
6	m.	d.	22	...	4,400,000	...	88	668
7	m.	d.	25	...	4,480,000	...	90	531
8	m.	d.	10	...	4,765,000	...	96	572
9	m.	d.	68	...	4,790,000	...	96	1052
10	m.	d.	90	...	4,892,000	...	97	670
11	m.	d.	11	...	4,918,000	...	98	893
12	m.	d.	31	...	4,929,000	...	99	750
13	m.	d.	22	...	4,981,000	...	99	681
14	m.	d.	34	...	5,006,000	...	100	1249
15	m.	d.	92	...	5,033,000	...	100	841
16	m.	d.	20	...	5,126,000	...	102	1027
17	m.	d.	15	...	5,210,000	...	104	507
18	m.	w.	83	...	5,311,000	...	106	771
				10	...	4,889,000	98	1038
19	m.	d.	91	...	5,514,000	...	110	701
20	m.	d.	60	...	5,730,000	...	114	1029
21	m.	d.	80	...	5,780,000	...	116	1174
22	m.	d.	80	...	5,896,000	...	118	574
				60	...	5,290,000	106	651
Average					4,750,000	...	95	...

TABLE III.—ENUMERATION OF BLOOD CORPUSCLES AND VALUE OF HAEMOGLOBIN.

Number, in order of corpuscular richness.	Sex—Male or Female.	Variety—Dry or Wet.	Number of days since kakké symptoms developed.	Number of days since previous enumeration.	Number of red corpuscles per cubic millimetre.		Number of red corpuscles per haemic unit, or per cent. of corpuscular richness.	Number of red corpuscles to one white.	Number of white corpuscles per haemic unit, in hundredths.	Per cent. of haemoglobin.	Value of individual corpuscle in haemoglobin, in per cent.	Equivalent in normal corpuscles,—that is corpuscles having 100 cent. haemoglobin.	
					First enumeration.	Subsequent enumeration.						Number of normal red corpuscles.	Per cent. of normal corpuscles.
1	f.p.	d.	22	...	1,795,000	...	36	131	.38	36	100	1,795,000	36
2	f.	d.	40	...	3,050,000	...	61	183	.33	82	120	3,660,000	73
3	f.p.	w.	30	...	3,320,000	...	66	365	.19	58	88	2,922,000	58
4	m.	d.	130	...	3,525,000	...	71	251	.27	58	82	2,890,000	58
5	m.	d.	20	...	3,555,000	...	71	960	.07	74	104	3,697,000	73
6	m.	d.	25	...	3,660,000	...	73	494	.15	62	85	3,111,000	62
7	f.	d.	30	...	3,660,000	...	73	593	.12	68	93	3,404,000	68
8	f.p.	d.	37	...	3,680,000	...	74	284	.27	56	76	2,897,000	58
9	m.	w.	40	...	3,780,000	...	76	1021	.07	58	76	2,853,000	57
10	f.p.	d.	15	...	3,795,000	...	76	410	.18	70	90	3,516,000	70
11	m.	w.	35	...	3,825,000	...	77	310	.25	78	101	3,863,000	77
12	m.	d.	98	...	3,879,000	...	78	524	.15	84	101	3,908,000	78
13	f.	w.	50	...	3,975,000	...	79	131	.57	60	76	3,079,000	63
14	f.	d.	11	...	4,005,000	...	80	260	.31	61	70	3,804,000	56
15	f.	d.	20	...	4,015,000	...	80	310	.26	94	117	4,698,000	94
16	m.	d.	135	...	4,065,000	...	81	489	.19	74	91	3,699,000	74
17	m.	d.	30	...	4,135,000	...	82	609	.14	90	112	4,630,000	93
18	f.p.	d.	35	...	4,160,000	...	83	631	.13	52	63	2,611,000	52
19	f.	d.	18	...	4,175,000	...	83	423	.20	71	85	3,549,000	71
20	m.	d.	85	...	4,190,000	...	84	857	.10	77	92	3,855,000	77
21	m.	d.	90	...	4,195,000	...	84	269	.31	64	76	3,187,000	64
22	m.	d.	20	...	4,215,000	...	84	1345	.06	72	86	3,624,000	73
23	f.p.	d.	35	...	4,225,000	...	84	684	.12	60	70	2,958,000	59
24	m.	d.	45	...	4,240,000	...	85	561	.15	91	107	4,357,000	91
25	m.	d.	20	...	4,250,000	...	85	608	.14	62	73	3,103,000	62
26	f.p.	d.	20	...	4,280,000	...	85	851	.10	62	73	3,124,000	62
27	m.	d.	60	...	4,316,000	...	86	259	.33	76	88	3,798,000	76
28	m.	d.	40	...	4,330,000	...	87	767	.11	80	92	3,984,000	80
29	m.	d.	55	...	4,340,000	...	87	564	.15	92	105	4,557,000	91
30	f.p.	d.	105	...	4,365,000	...	87	631	.15	64	73	3,186,000	64
				29	...	4,235,000	86	424	.20	86	100	...	...
31	m.	d.	12	...	4,365,000	...	87	505	.18	58	66	2,771,000	56
32	f.p.	d.	145	...	4,395,000	...	88	1007	.09	72	82	3,614,000	72
33	m.	d.	15	...	4,435,000	...	89	513	.17	88	99	4,391,000	88
34	m.	d.	36	...	4,445,000	...	89	267	.30	86	100	4,445,000	89
35	m.	d.	75	...	4,480,000	...	90	1209	.07	78	77	3,450,000	69
36	f.p.	d.	40	...	4,505,000	...	90	1042	.08	76	80	3,804,000	76
37	m.	d.	60	...	4,510,000	...	90	985	.09	80	89	4,014,000	80
				58	...	5,110,000	102	526	.19	96	94	...	...
38	m.	w.	20	...	4,510,000	...	90	627	.14	82	91	4,104,000	82
39	f.p.	d.	50	...	4,520,000	...	90	508	.18	79	88	4,418,000	88
40	m.	d.	40	...	4,566,000	...	91	566	.16	80	89	4,464,000	89
41	f.	d.	15	...	4,575,000	...	92	562	.16	70	76	3,477,000	70
				17	...	4,700,000	94	846	.11	66	70	...	...
42	f.p.	d.	60	...	4,595,000	...	92	355	.26	68	74	3,400,000	68
43	m.	d.	35	...	4,625,000	...	93	834	.11	76	82	4,082,000	82
44	m.	d.	90	...	4,635,000	...	93	936	.10	78	94	4,357,000	87

STUDIES IN JAPANESE "KAKKÉ," OR BERIBERI.

45	m.	d.	40	...	4,685,000	...	93	578	.17	76	82	3,791,000	76
46	m.	d.	40	...	4,665,000	...	93	581	.16	76	82	3,825,000	77
47	m.	d.	10	...	4,730,000	...	94	590	.16	98	103	4,872,000	97
48	m.	d.	15	...	4,800,000	...	96	598	.16	74	77	3,696,000	74
49	m.	d.	15	...	4,815,000	...	96	592	.16	89	95	4,574,000	91
50	f.	d.	80	...	4,820,000	...	96	446	.22	70	73	3,519,000	71
51	m.	d.	24	...	4,855,000	...	97	518	.19	84	87	4,224,000	84
52	m.	d.	11	...	4,875,000	...	98	1052	.09	84	88	4,390,000	88
53	m.	d.	7	...	4,900,000	...	98	496	.20	78	80	3,920,000	78
54	m.	d.	151	...	4,965,000	...	99	540	.18	79	88	4,369,000	87
55	m.	d.	60	...	4,970,000	...	99	344	.26	80	80	3,976,000	80
				22	...	5,175,000	103	1665	.06	84	82	...	...
56	f.p.	d.	60	...	4,980,000	...	99	536	.18	67	67	3,337,000	67
			74	14	...	5,210,000	104	1064	.09	62	60	...	...
			156	82	...	4,880,000	98	459	.21	74	75	...	...
			256	100	...	4,850,000	97	670	.14	76	78	...	...
			348	92	...	4,110,000	82	605	.14	64	78	...	...
57	m.	d.	95	...	4,980,000	...	99	576	.17	82	82	4,088,000	82
58	m.	d.	17	...	4,985,000	...	100	544	.18	82	82	4,387,000	88
59	m.	d.	65	...	4,985,000	...	100	385	.26	88	88	4,453,000	89
60	m.	d.	100	...	5,000,000	...	100	675	.15	98	98	4,900,000	98
61	m.	d.	25	...	5,060,000	...	101	387	.26	89	88	3,417,000	68
62	m.	d.	259	...	5,060,000	...	101	543	.18	92	91	4,605,000	92
63	m.	d.	...	...	5,090,000	...	102	825	.12	84	82	4,174,000	80
64	m.	d.	80	...	5,100,000	...	102	510	.20	92	90	4,590,000	92
65	m.	d.	14	...	5,100,000	...	102	846	.12	69	67	3,417,000	68
66	m.	d.	20	...	5,115,000	...	102	1033	.10	88	86	4,399,000	88
67	m.	d.	20	...	5,125,000	...	102	422	.24	72	69	3,536,000	71
68	m.	d.	20	...	5,160,000	...	103	464	.22	100	97	5,160,000	103
69	m.	d.	10	...	5,165,000	...	103	1130	.09	84	80	4,132,000	83
70	m.	d.	3	...	5,175,000	...	103	699	.15	89	86	4,451,000	89
71	m.	d.	295	...	5,210,000	...	104	470	.22	103	99	5,048,000	101
72	m.	w.	7	...	5,225,000	...	104	334	.31	98	94	4,912,000	98
73	m.	d.	58	...	5,230,000	...	105	1807	.06	88	84	4,493,000	90
74	m.	d.	20	...	5,235,000	...	105	480	.22	80	77	4,031,000	81
75	m.	d.	12	...	5,235,000	...	105	291	.36	72	69	3,602,000	72
76	m.	d.	12	...	5,235,000	...	105	567	.18	104	100	5,235,000	105
77	m.	d.	110	...	5,235,000	...	105	1412	.07	90	86	4,502,000	90
78	m.	d.	160	...	5,295,000	...	106	477	.22	104	97	5,136,000	103
79	m.	d.	30	...	5,300,000	...	106	715	.15	80	76	4,028,000	81
80	f.	d.	100	...	5,305,000	...	106	576	.19	82	77	4,085,000	82
81	m.	d.	70	...	5,305,000	...	106	949	.11	78	70	4,714,000	74
82	m.	d.	18	...	5,305,000	...	106	408	.26	96	90	3,775,000	96
83	m.	d.	30	...	5,315,000	...	106	488	.21	82	77	4,092,000	82
				33	...	4,140,000	83	976	.09	78	94	...	...
84	m.	d.	30	...	5,330,000	...	107	538	.20	90	86	4,780,000	96
85	m.	d.	125	...	5,335,000	...	107	633	.17	89	82	4,375,000	88
86	m.	d.	13	...	5,370,000	...	107	791	.14	90	84	4,520,000	91
87	m.	d.	26	...	5,375,000	...	107	652	.16	99	92	4,025,000	81
88	m.	d.	50	...	5,375,000	...	107	584	.19	82	76	4,095,000	82
89	m.	d.	30	...	5,385,000	...	107	969	.11	92	86	4,631,000	93
90	m.	d.	42	...	5,440,000	...	109	541	.20	64	59	3,160,000	63
			84	42	...	4,805,000	96	520	.18	76	79	...	...
			138	54	...	4,950,000	99	527	.18	78	79	...	...
			242	104	...	4,475,000	90	375	.24	64	71	...	...
			325	83	...	4,400,000	88	600	.15	66	75	...	...
91	m.	d.	100	...	5,530,000	...	111	1289	.09	92	83	4,590,000	92
92	m.	d.	13	...	5,585,000	...	111	524	.21	96	86	4,750,000	95
93	m.	d.	60	...	5,585,000	...	111	651	.17	102	96	5,814,000	106

94	m.	d.	162	...	5,725,000	...	114	633	.18	94	82	4,695,000	94
95	m.	d.	9	...	5,775,000	...	115	459	.25	90	78	4,505,000	90
			30	21	...	4,845,000	97	1043	.09	86	89	...	...
			51	21	...	6,055,000	121	1118	.10	91	84	...	...
			163	112	...	5,050,000	101	724	.14	86	85	...	...
			282	119	...	5,045,000	101	628	.16	96	95	...	...
96	m.	d.	40	...	5,920,000	...	118	413	.28	83	70	4,144,000	83
97	m.	d.	20	...	5,930,000	...	119	1067	.11	85	71	4,210,000	84
98	m.	d.	55	...	6,020,000	...	120	610	.20	88	73	4,395,000	88
99	m.	d.	293	...	6,090,000	...	122	731	.17	116	95	5,786,000	106
100	m.	d.	170	...	6,110,000	...	122	741	.17	100	82	5,010,000	100
101	m.	d.	10	...	6,145,000	...	123	1657	.07	94	75	4,609,000	90
Average					4,626,000	...	93	...	...	81	...	4,124,000	83

In numerating the blood corpuscles both Hayem and Nachet's Haematometre and Dr. Gower's Haemacytometer were used. In those cases given in tables I. and II. Nachet's instrument was used; and Gower's Haemacytometer and Haemoglobinometer in table III. In using Nachet's instrument the red corpuscles in from 9 to 12 large squares were counted, and the white corpuscles in from 45 to 60 large squares. In using Dr. Gower's instrument the red corpuscles in from 20 to 30 squares were counted, and the white in from 150 to 200 squares. The cover glasses used were those furnished by each maker respectively, using the same cover till it was broken and then taking another. No pains was taken to use the same side of the cover up. The Gower's instrument used was tested at the Kew observatory. Nachet's instrument was assured by the maker to be absolutely correct, and in comparing it with Gower's, using the same specimen of blood, I found no essential difference.

The cases are arranged in the tables in the order of their corpuscular richness, commencing with the lowest.

In table III. in the column sex, "f.p." denotes puerperal female. The "No. of normal red corpuscles," in next to the right hand column, was obtained by multiplying the number of red corpuscles in each case by the value of the individual corpuscle in haemoglobin in that case.

It will be seen from these tables that there is a slight degree of anaemia in kakké. The average corpuscular richness for the 134 cases given in the tables is 94 per cent. This corresponds with clinical experience in cases of kakké. Most of the cases of kakké seen by the general practitioner are well fed, well nourished, full blooded appearing men. The ill fed, poorly nourished, weak constitution kakké cases are the exception. During the last few years I have kept a record of the physical condition of the kakké patients seen, and herewith give a summary of that record, together with a similar report of a kakké hospital in Tokiyo:—

	Taylor.	Kakké hospital	Sum.
Of strong constitution	323	593	916
„ average „	15	27	42
„ weak „	9	6	15

Thus in a total of 973 kakké patients there was 94 per cent. of strong constitution (a result almost identical with that given in the above tables) and only 6 per cent. of average and weak constitutions. These numbers are large enough to be conclusive, and anaemia is not one of the pathological conditions of kakké. In those cases where there was some anaemia, no relation was found to exist between the amount of anaemia and the severity of the disease. The palor and oedema of the face so often seen in cases of kakké is deceptive, giving the patient an anaemic appearance when no anaemia exists.

The tables show (with but few exceptions) no increase in the white blood corpuscles.

Table III. shows a general diminution of the haemoglobin. The average haemoglobin in the 101 cases is 81 per cent. In some of these cases the amount is very low, being below 65 per cent., and with but few exceptions the per cent. of haemoglobin is below the per cent. of corpuscles, showing a deficiency of the individual corpuscles in haemoglobin. Though a deficiency of haemoglobin thus appears to be one of the pathological conditions of kakké, yet I found no relation existing between the deficiency of haemoglobin and the severity of the disease.

The clinical record of the cases here given shows that the most of those cases where marked anaemia existed, were associated with deranged digestion or complicated with other blood impoverishing diseases. Marked anaemia in cases of kakké not thus complicated are exceptional, but there is a slight degree of anaemia in most cases of kakké that have continued for some time.

III.—CONDITION OF THE CIRCULATION.

The condition of the circulation is one of the most striking as well as the most important features of kakké. However profound the muscular paralysis may be, there is no occasion for alarm so long as the respiratory and circulatory systems are not involved. But in most cases of marked muscular paralysis the respiratory muscles are somewhat weakened, and the circulatory system seriously affected. The phenomena of "*Shiyoshin*"*—which is liable to suddenly occur at any time in any case—is chiefly due to failure of the circulation and respiration, especially the former. I have witnessed but few cases of death from kakké where failure of the circulation was not the chief, and in many instances the sole, cause of death. Though these paroxysms of "*shiyoshin*" sometimes unexpectedly and suddenly occur in mild cases, yet they are generally preceded by a gradual failure of the powers of circulation; and the judicious physician must look to the condition of the circulation for the first indication of serious consequence to his patient.

For the purpose of more fully studying the cardiac and vascular phenomena occurring in kakké I began a series of observations† with the Sphygmograph,‡ and give herewith some

---

* "*Shiyoshin*."—This term as used by the Japanese has no pathological signification; they simply mean by it a metastasis of kakké to the chest. The paroxysms of "*Shiyoshin*" bear some resemblance to an acute attack of *Angina pectoris*. There is great distress in the chest, accompanied by marked dyspnoea, and failure of the powers of circulation. The action of the heart is sometimes rapid and violent, and again it is calm and quiet. But whatever be the character of the heart's action, the increased feebleness of the pulse and increased blueness of the extremities show a marked diminution of circulatory power. These paroxysms are almost invariably the precursors of a fatal termination. The patient not infrequently dies in the first paroxysm; he may linger, however, a few days, the paroxysms growing more and more frequent and severe till death ends the distressing scene.

† A full report of these observations are published in the *Tokei Medical Journal*, 1885-6.

‡ The tracings here given were taken with Marey's Sphygmograph, improved by Mahomed; and the rate of travel by the slide bearing the card was from 11 to 12 *cm.* in 10 seconds. Pond's instrument, furnished me, exaggerated slight deviations from the normal, and could not be used where precision was required. The tracings taken with this instrument and here given are so designated.

---

of the cases with the tracings taken during the summers of 1883 and 84.

In the description given of these cases I confine myself to a statement of those symptoms which have a bearing upon the circulation.

1.—SLIGHT CARDIAC DEBILITY.

Case 1. K.— *Male, aet.* 31.*

Patient is of strong constitution, has now been ill with kakké 40 days. He suffers chiefly in the legs. He can squat and rise up with difficulty, and by an effort can stand on tip-toe. He can walk a short distance with comfort, but if he attempts to walk fast, or any distance, he suffers from palpitation of the heart and is compelled to stop.

Condition of blood, Table III.—No. 45.
Dynamometer, R.H. 110 (outer circle).
     L.H. 102   „
Resp. 26. Pulse, 82. The pulse feels soft yet it is somewhat incompressible, and its stroke partakes somewhat of the "water-hammer" character. It is not weakened if the arm is elevated above the head. The aortic and pulmonary valve sounds are normal; so also are the other heart sounds.

Tracing 1. (See tracings at end of book).

These tracings were taken with the patient sitting by a table. Pressure of each, 2 oz. After the upper tracing was taken, the patient walked around the square, and came back short of breath, saying he was suffering from palpitation of the heart. The second tracing was at once taken, but shows but little change from the first.

The dyspnoea and cardiac palpitation which this man suffered on slight exertion indicated some weakness of the heart, but the sphygmographic tracings show that the heart is not seriously affected.

Case 2. I.—T. *Male, aet.* 35.

This patient is of average constitution, and has been ill with kakké for 15 days. He has a pale, waxy countenance, with some pigmentation, and appears feeble, but says he is in no distress. He walks across the room perfectly with a staggering gait. He cannot squat down, nor rise up, nor stand on tip-toe, nor even raise his heels from the floor in the effort.

Condition of blood, Table III.—No. 33.
Dynm. R.H. 60, L.H. 50.
Pulse, standing, 70; after walking across the room, 80. Resp. 16. The pulse feels full

---

* See Addenda,—Age.

and soft, but imparts to the finger a sense as if the blood flowed along the artery by floods, to be completely emptied during the cardiac diastole. Elevating the arm above the head does not affect the pulse. The aortic valve sound is less distinct than the pulmonary. The apex sound is forcible, somewhat "water-hammer" like. The chest does not heave.

Trac. 2. (———)

These tracings were taken with the patient sitting by a table. Pressure, 2 oz. After taking the upper tracing the patient walked back and forth across the room two or three times, when the lower tracing was taken.

Seven days later tracings were again taken. In the mean time the patient had been taking digitalis and felt much more comfortable after slight exercise. He does not now suffer from palpitation.

Trac. 3. (———)

These tracings were taken under the same conditions that the previous tracings were. Pressure of the upper tracing, 1 oz.; of the lower, 2 oz.

Tracings 2 show very sudden systole, with condition in diastolic period irregular. Slight exercise brings out more forcibly the irregular action of the heart. Tracings 3 show but little improvement, while the condition of the patient was very much more comfortable after slight exercise. The muscles of the legs were thrown into a violent quiver on slight exertion, and the patient was suffering somewhat from general nervous prostration, but the cardiac muscles were less affected than those of the lower extremities.

Case 3. I.—Om. Female,[*] aet. 34.

The patient is of good constitution, she has now been ill 20 days. This is a case complicated with pneumonia; the pneumonia commencing first, and kakké set in afterwards. She cannot rise up nor stand, she can, however, *suwari*[†] with difficulty. She can imperfectly flex and extend the legs, feet and toes. The grasp of the hand is very weak. She can raise her arms up but cannot extend the fingers. Pulse 60, and if an effort to rise up is made the pulse at once runs up to 85. She suffers much from distress in the chest, and palpitation of the heart; and if an effort is made these are very much increased. The pulse feels strong and full with a hammer-like stroke. The heart sounds are normal.

Condition of blood, Table II.—No. 4.

Trac. 4. (———)

These tracings were taken with the patient lying down. Pressure of the upper tracing 1 oz. and of the lower 4 oz.

These tracings show a favorable condition of the heart and good tension of the circulation. With this woman's distress in the chest, marked dyspnœa, and extensive muscular paralysis, I felt apprehensive for the result, but the sphygmographic tracings assured me there was no immediate danger. She soon began to improve, and in a short time was up and around.

Case 4. M.—Male, aet. 44.

This patient is of strong constitution, and has now been ill with kakké about 50 days. This is the ninth successive[*] year he has had kakké. He can walk a short distance without inconvenience, but if he attempts to walk any distance or to walk fast he suffers from dyspnœa, palpitation of the heart, distress in the chest, and is compelled to rest. If quiet he suffers no inconvenience. The upper extremities are not affected. The pulse and heart sounds are normal.

Trac. 5. (———)

This tracing was taken with the patient sitting at a table. Pulse 70, pressure 4 oz. The systolic upstroke shows a somewhat sudden percussion. This is characteristic in kakké where the heart is but slightly affected. The tension of the circulation is good, however. I encouraged the man to keep on with his work (he was a doctor), but not to attempt to walk.

The year before when this man had kakké, the muscular paralysis was mild, but the heart was exceedingly weak. He could not walk more than a few steps without suffering such distress in the chest, dyspnœa and palpitation of the heart, that he was compelled at once to lie down. The chest would palpitate and quiver under the violent and irregular action of the heart. He could not even rise up to *suwari* or stand without distressing disturbance of the heart. I kept him lying quiet in bed for over two months. But not having an instrument at my command at the time, I was unable to take a tracing.

---

[*] See Addenda.—Sex.
[†] *Suwari*, to sit in the Japanese position.

[*] See Addenda,—Recurrence.

Case 5. *M—T—. Male, aet.* 41.

The patient is of strong constitution. This man has had kakké seven summers within the last ten years. This is the fifth successive year he has suffered from kakké, and he has now been ill three months. Atrophy is quite marked. He cannot stand, nor squat down, nor rise up on his feet. Dynam. R. H. 25., L. H. 25. He is troubled somewhat with palpitation of the heart and slight distress in the chest. Pulse, 98 ; feels weak to the touch. The heart sounds are feebly heard, but otherwise normal.

Urine scant.* Condition of blood, Table III. —No. 21.

Trac. 6. (———)

This tracing was taken with the patient lying down. Pressure, 4 oz. This is a good tracing, and shows the heart in good condition. It is in striking contrast with the feeble muscular condition of the patient.

This series of cases is instructive in showing the condition of the heart and circulation when the circulatory system is but slightly affected. The general practitioner meets a large number of cases of kakké, where there is but slight muscular paralysis, and anaesthesia of the lower extremities, muscular hyperasthesia and slight oedema may be either present or absent, but with no evidence of cardiac weakness. Again a large number of mild cases are complicated with slight cardiac debility, as in cases 1 and 4. The patient is comfortable if he remains quiet, and the heart is able to meet the demands laid upon it without showing special weakness. The sphygmograph tracing also does not deviate much from the normal ; but if the patient puts forth moderate effort, he soon commences to suffer fron cardiac dyspnoea and palpitation of the heart ; this slight physical exertion lays an additional burden upon the heart which in its debilitated condition it is not able to meet, and it shows its weakness by irregular and laborious action. The character of the cardiac weakness is seen not to be that of valvular lesion but of nervous or muscular weakness.

In case 2 the muscular and cardiac weakness is much the same. The heart can meet without showing special disturbance all the increased labor the debilitated muscles are capable of throwing upon it. While the cardiac debility remained the same, if the muscles were stronger, so as to throw more labor on the heart by exercise, we could bring out more decidedly the heart weakness. The condition of the circulation is seen to be irregular during the diastolic period, and the dicrotic wave subject to considerable variation, so that in addition to cardiac debility, there is low tension and evidence of diminished arterial tone.

In cases 3 and 4 the muscular paralysis, especially of the lower extremities, was quite marked, but not complete, while the heart and circulation was in a good condition.

2.—IRREGULAR ACTION OF HEART.

Case 4. *Y.—Male, aet.* 26.

The patient is of strong constitution. He is not able to either stand nor sit up. Dynm. R. H. 20., L. H. 20. There is marked paralysis, especially of the lower extremities.

Temp. 38.8° C., Resp. 30., Pulse variable, from 65 to 80. The pulse feels strong though irregular ; occasionally there is a weak beat, sometimes a remission. The pulse is not weakened if the arm is elevated, neither is the click of the aortic cusps weakened. There is a systolic *bruit* at the apex.

Condition of blood, Table III.—No. 31.

This man had been ill with kakké for some time, when typhoid fever set in. During the second week of the fever the pulse became very irregular, and I became apprehensive of the final result, when the tracing was taken.

Trac. 7. (———)

Under the influence of strychnia, digitalis and whiskey, after a few days, the pulse began to improve.

This tracing is by no means the pulse tracing of a pure kakké case. Irregular action of the heart is frequently met with in pure kakké cases, but the variation of the pulse-trace is of a different character. Such a variation is shown in tracings 13 and 27, and cardiac tracings 37, 38 and 39.

3.—EFFECTS OF VARYING PRESSURE.

Case 7. *Y.—Male, aet.* 27.

The patient is of good constitution. Can walk imperfectly across the room and back. Dynm. R. H. 40., L. H. 38. Patient is troubled some with dyspnoea, and palpitation of the heart.

Trac. 8. (———)

These tracings were taken with the patient lying down. Pulse, 98 ; Resp. 30. The pulse is not weakened if the arm is elevated. The

---

* See Addenda,—Urine.

click of the aortic cusps is full; there is a *bruit* over the pulmonary valves. The action of the heart is forcible and laborious. The pressure of the upper tracing was 2 oz., of the second 4 oz., and of the lower 6 oz. A pressure of 8 oz. about cut off vibration of the lever. The points to be noticed in these tracings are the tall and forcible up-stroke during the systole and the *hyperdicrotic pulse*.

Case 8. *O.—S. Male, aet.* 16.

The patient is of strong constitution, and has now been ill 35 days. Anaesthesia is slight, muscular paralysis quite marked. He cannot rise up nor stand. He can move the feet and legs. Dynm. R. H. 18., L. H. 20. Condition of blood, Table III.—No. 43.

Trac. 9. (——)

These tracings were taken with the patient lying down. Pulse, 96. If the arm is elevated the pulse is slightly weakened. Heart sounds normal. The extremities of the fingers and toes feel cold, and have a marked palor, but not the least purple hue. Pressure of the upper tracing 2 oz., of the middle $3\frac{1}{4}$ oz., and of the lower 5 oz. A pressure of 7 oz. cuts off all vibration of the lever. These tracings show an empty condition of the arteries during ventricular diastole and a weak heart. The patient is eminently in danger of an attack of "*shiyoshin.*"

Case 9. *K. O N. Female, aet.* 41.

Patient is of strong constitution. This is a case of puerperal* kakké. She gave birth to a child 35 days ago. There was much oedema before child-birth, but no symptoms of kakké. The oedema continued to increase after the birth of the child, and kakké symptoms began some five days after she was confined. This is the tenth successive year she has suffered from kakké.

Condition of blood, Table III.—No. 16.

She cannot stand, nor can she raise her legs off the bed; she can move her legs, however, but cannot move herself in bed. Dynm. R.H. 5, L.H. 2. The voice is thin and weak from lack of respiratory force. There is partial paralysis of the diaphraghm, and the inspirations are feeble. Urine scant, about 575 cc. in 24 hours.

Trac. 10. (——)

These tracings were taken with the patient

---

* See Addenda,—Puerperal kakké.

lying down. Pulse 80, and weak. The weakness does not appear to be increased by elevating the arm. The click of the aortic cusps is about the same as that of the pulmonary. The pressure of the upper tracing was 1 oz., of the second 3 oz., of the third 5 oz., and of the lowest tracing $6\frac{1}{3}$ oz. A pressure of 8 oz. checked all vibration of the lever.

The *heart wave* in this tracing shows a weak heart; the grasp of the ventricle upon the contained blood is weakened at the close of the systole, and no amount of pressure sharpens up the apex of the percussion wave. Such tracings as this (and in a measure we may include trac. 9) are not often met with in kakké, and though they show marked cardiac weakness, they do not lead to so grave a prognosis as where *dicrotism* is more fully marked.

In cases of kakké a light pressure of from 1 to 3 oz. generally produces the best tracings. A pressure of 4 or more ounces, while it cuts off the height of the percussion stroke, fails to improve the tracing or develop latent points.

4.—Effects of Exercise.

Case 10. *U.— Male, aet.* 19.

The patient is of strong constitution, and has been ill for 20 days. The anaesthesia and muscular paralysis is but slight. He complains of palpitation of the heart on slight exercise, and inability to walk on this account. Pulse 94, is full and strong, is slightly weakened if the arm is elevated. The heart sounds are normal, and there is no praecordial pulsation.

Trac. 11. (——)

These tracings were taken with the patient sitting at a table. The upper tracing was taken before exercise, pressure 1 oz. Then the second tracing, with a varying pressure of 2 then 4 oz. A pressure of $5\frac{1}{4}$ oz. cut off all movement of the lever. The patient then walked around the square and after a few minutes' delay the third tracing was taken; pressure 2 oz.

The noticeable points of these tracings are the tall upstroke and the precipitous fall from the apex of the percussion wave, indicating the strong shock communicated by the grasp of the ventricle upon the contained blood and the collapsed condition of the arteries immediately succeeding the vigorous ventricular systole. This points to a weakened *vaso-motor* system, with relaxed arteries and veins and a free outflow through the capillaries. Exercise has improved the tracing; not that the condition of the circulatory system has been improved by the exercise, but the more vigorous action of the heart has filled up the relaxed arterial system which now shows more tension. In this condition of the heart and arteries, the circulatory system would collapse under the increased strain of moderate exercise continued for a time. This is a very common condition in kakké.

Case 11. M.—S. Male, aet. 20.

The patient is of strong constitution, and has been ill 25 days. For a time he was so bad his doctor despaired of his life. At present he has somewhat improved, and can hobble across the room. He cannot squat nor rise up, nor stand on tip-toe. He has suffered much from distress in the chest and palpitation of the heart. By using his hands to aid himself in rising up and then walking a very few steps, very much increases the cardiac palpitation and the distress in the chest. While he remains quiet he is comfortable. Pulse 100, and appears normal to the touch, but is weakened by elevating the arm. The heart sounds are normal. There is no praecordial pulsation. The hands and feet are cold. Dynm. R. H. 95, L. H. 100.

Condition of blood, Table III.—No. 6.

Trac. 12. (——)

These tracings were taken with the patient *suwari-ing* by a low form. The upper tracing was taken before exercise; pressure, 3½ oz. Then the patient steadied himself by placing his hand on my shoulder and walked across the room and back, when the second tracing was taken. Some little time was lost in properly adjusting the instrument. Pressure, 2½ oz. Then the patient again walked across the room and back, while the instrument was steadied on his arm, and at once the lower tracing was taken. Pressure, 1 oz.

There is not much difference between the upper and lower tracings. There is increased tremor during the diastole of the second tracing, and both tracings show low tension of the circulation. The third tracing shows increased suddenness and force of ventricular contraction, with precipitous fall from apex of percussion wave, and marked dicrotism. These have all been increased by exercise. If the muscles of the lower extremities were stronger, so as to allow the patient to take more exercise, the muscular weakness of the heart could be more fully brought out, yet in their present debilitated condition the heart and arterial system would not allow of greater strain being thrown upon them. Here in addition to the paralysis of the lower extremities we evidently have partial muscular paralysis of the heart and diminished *vaso-motor* power.

Case 12. F.—H. Male, aet. 35.

The patient is of strong constitution, and has now been ill about 90 days. During this time he has been better and worse several times. He is now much better than he has been for several weeks. He can walk a few blocks comfortably, but after that he becomes weary and is troubled with palpitation of the heart and distress in the chest.

Dynm. R. H. 80, L. H. 85.

Condition of blood, Table III.—No. 44.

Temp. 38.3° C. Resp. 22. Pulse, 90. The pulse feels strong and full to the touch, but not natural. The sensation imparted to the finger is as if a flood of blood flowed along the artery at each ventricular stroke, and was then immediately emptied till the next beat. If the arm is elevated above the head the pulse is weakened. The click of the aortic cusps is fainter than the pulmonary. There is praecordial pulsation, and the impact of the apex stroke is seen more prominently 3 cm. to the left and 3 cm. below the left nipple. The first sound is loudest over the normal position when the patient sits up, and at the seat of greatest impulse when he lies down. The apex is not tilted. There is some general oedema. The area of cardiac dulness is enlarged downward and to the left. There is evidently some effusion into the pericardium. After rising up and walking across the room the pulse is increased to 100. The tracings were taken with the patient *suwari-ing* beside a low form.

Trac. 13. (——)

After the first tracing was taken the patient walked around the square, and came back short of breath, suffering from palpitation of the heart and in considerable distress. There was some delay in properly adjusting the instrument, when the second, third and fourth tracings were taken as rapidly as the cards could be changed and the instrument started. When the patient first came in from this exercise the pulse was 160; when the second tracing was taken it was 140, and the action of the heart violent, with a "water-hammer" like stroke. The pulse rapidly diminished, the patient became blanched, and was about to fall over, when he was laid down and the instrument removed from his arm.

Pressure of the first and second tracings 2½ oz., of the third 3 oz., and of the last 2½ oz.

Seven days later the next series of tracings

was taken. In the mean time the patient had been taking cathartics, diuretics, digitalis and small doses of strychnia. The general oedema was much reduced, the effusion into the pericardium removed, and the impulse of the apex stroke is found to-day in the normal position. There is coldness and palor of the extremities, but no purple hue. Pulse, 100.

Trac. 14. (———)

These tracings were taken with the patient *suwari-ing* by a low form. The first tracing was taken before exercise, pressure 3 oz. Then the patient walked around the room a few times, and after the delay of a few minutes the second tracing was taken. The instrument was then held in place while the patient walked around the room twice, and immediately on *suwari-ing* down the last tracing was taken.

The first series of tracings (trac. 13), show the very sudden impulse imparted to the lever, marking the exaggerated momentum of the ventricular systole, the precipitous fall from the apex of the percussion wave, the irregular action of the heart, and the pronounced but irregular respiratory wave. Exercise exaggerates all these deviations from the normal. The second series of tracings show a slight improvement, but are of the same general character.

The tracings after exercise in the first series and immediately after exercise in the second series, show with what excited and irregular action the heart in its weakened condition responds to the demands of increased activity enforced by slight exercise. The second tracing in the last series shows that the heart in its weakened condition after being forced into increased activity by even slight exercise, rapidly falls into a state of comparative repose (see also trac. 16). If the strain thrown upon the heart in this condition is somewhat prolonged, this reaction may develop into a fatal collapse. This man on two different occasions had been made much worse by trotting to the post office just before the closure of the mail. On one occasion two of my patients who were up and attending to business, were made so much worse by a short run on the alarm of fire that they were compelled to keep their beds for several weeks.

The reaction after prolonged though gentle exercise may be delayed some hours, but in this weakened condition of the heart it is sure to come. I have several times had my patients made so much worse by being gently carried to the mountains, when the heart was in a feeble condition, that before morning their lives were despaired of and were in a very critical condition for several days. I never give my consent to the removal of a patient showing marked cardiac weakness. Last summer two of my patients saw proper to disregard my advice to remain quiet within doors and went out to attend to business, the one riding in a jinrikisha, and the other taking the cars to Kobe. Both were attacked with *shiyoshin* a few hours after returning, one died before morning and the other within 24 hours. I recollect being called in counsel in two cases, where the kakké symptoms were so slight that they were disregarded, and the men had walked a considerable distance the preceding day. They both spent an uncomfortable night, and *shiyoshin* developed the next morning, the one dying almost immediately, and the other within three hours. While there is marked *vaso-motor* debility, and the heart is suffering from partial muscular paralysis. as it frequently does in cases of kakké, there is no security but in enforced rest.

5.—WEAKNESS PREDICTING "SHIYOSHIN."

Case 13. T.—R.—Male, aet. 28.

The patient is of strong constitution, and has now been ill about 50 days. He can walk a short distance, can squat, but can rise up only with great difficulty, can only partially rise on tip-toe. Dynm. R. H. 58., L. H. 60.

Condition of blood, Table III.—No. 16.

He feels comfortable while still, but slight exertion produces palpitation of the heart and distress in the chest. Pulse 112, and feels normal to the touch, but is slightly weakened if the arm is elevated above the head. The click of the aortic cusps is weaker than that of the pulmonary; otherwise the heart sounds are normal. There is strong praecordial pulsation, and the chest trembles under the toiling action of the heart.

Trac. 15. (———)

The tracings were taken with the patient sitting by a table. Pressure of the upper tracing 1 oz., of the second 4 oz. Then the patient walked back and forth across the room a few times, when the last tracing was taken, but the distance walked was too short to produce any special change in the action of the heart. Pressure 3 oz.

This tracing shows very sudden impulse with full discrotism, but is not more indicative of "*shiyoshin*" than either tracings 11 or 14.

Case 14. *N.—O Y. Female, aet.* 26.

Patient is of average constitution, and has been ill for 28 days. She walks with some effort, she can squat but cannot rise up, nor can she stand on tip-toe, but can raise her heels from the floor in the effort. Dynm. R. H. 82, L. H. 78.

Condition of blood, Table III.—No. 7.

Temp. 37.7° C., Resp. 18, Pulse 126, and peculiar. It remits once in every 40 or 50 beats, and then follow three or four rapid and confused pulsations. The pulse is not weakened if the arm is elevated. These tracings were taken with the patient *suwari-ing* by a low form. Pressure of the first 1 oz., of the second 2 oz., and of the last 3 oz.

Trac. 16. (——)

After taking the first tracing the patient steadied herself by placing her hand on my shoulder and walked across the room and back. Some little time was lost in adjusting the instrument, when the second tracing was taken. The instrument was then held in place on her arm while she walked across the room and back, steadying herself as before by placing her hand on my shoulder, and at once the third tracing was taken.

The action of the heart is seen to be irregular, the pulse is fully dicrotic, with marked respiratory curves. The patient was ordered to keep the recumbent position, and her friends informed that "*shiyoshin*" might develop at any time.

Case 15. *M. Male, aet.* 40.

The patient is of strong constitution, and has now been ill 25 days. He cannot stand nor *suwari*. He can slightly move his legs, but cannot raise his legs off the bed. He can partially turn himself in bed. He can raise his arms, but the wrist of the left arm drops and he cannot raise it. He can partially extend the fingers of the right hand, but cannot in the least extend the fingers of the left hand. Dynm. R.H. 5, L.H. 0.

Condition of blood, Table II.—No. 7.

Temp. 38.2° C. Pulse, 110. He suffers some from palpitation of the heart and has some distress in the chest. To the touch the pulse feels normal, but when the arm is raised the pulse is very much weakened. As the patient lies on his back I cannot detect the click of either the aortic or pulmonary cusps. By turning the patient slightly on his left side I can distinguish the pulmonary valve sound but not the aortic. The first sound of the heart is normal over the apex, but is flattened over the right side of the heart. There is no praecordial pulsation, nor is the action of the heart labored. The extremities of the hands and feet are cold and blanched, but not in the least pigmented, yet the finger nails are slightly purple.

Trac. 17. (——)

These tracings were taken with the patient lying on his back. Pressure of the upper tracing 3 oz., and of the lower 4 oz. The tracings show a hyperdicrotic pulse, and exhibit greater cardiac and *vaso-motor* weakness than the general condition of the patient would lead us to infer. The tracing showed the patient to be in eminent danger, and "*shiyoshin*" liable to develop at any time.

The patient was put on large doses of digitalis and small doses of strychnia, and soon began to show some improvement. Eleven days later we found the paralysis of the right leg had improved, while that of the left had grown worse. He can raise the arms, but the wrists drop. He can raise the wrist of the right arm, but not the left. He can extend the fingers of both hands to-day, and the strength of the flexors has considerably improved. Dynm. R. H. 18, L. H. 8. Pulse, 90, and to the touch it feels normal, but if the arm is elevated it is weakened. The click of the aortic and pulmonary cusps are faintly audible as the patient lies on his back. The general oedema has increased. As the patient lies on his back slightly inclined to the left side, the greatest impulse of the apex beat is felt 4 cm. to the left of the left nipple, and the greatest intensity of the beat is heard at this point. But when the patient is propped up in the *suwari* position, the point of greatest impulse is just below the nipple, and the beat is heard with greatest intensity at this point. There is praecordial pulsation, increased dulness to the left side, with effusion into the pericardium. The hands and feet are cold, but in a better condition than when last seen.

Trac. 18. (——)

These tracings were taken with the patient lying on his back. Pressure of the upper tracing 1 oz., and of the second 3 oz. These tracings show a favorable improvement compared with those previously taken. The patient was pronounced out of danger, notwithstanding the increased oedema. Each of these three cases after a time fully recovered.

Case 16. K. T. Male, aet. 49.

The patient is of strong constitution. This is his fifth attack of kakké, and he has now been ill 35 days. He cannot stand, neither can he flex or extend either his legs or feet. He can slightly move the toes and imperfectly rotate the legs. His wrists drop when the arms are raised, and he cannot raise them, nor can he fully extend the fingers. Dynm. R. H. 5, L. H. 5.

Condition of blood, Table III.—No. 11.

Resp. 26. Pulse weak, and is more weakened when the arm is elevated. I cannot distinguish the click of either the aortic or pulmonary cusps, as the patient lies on his back, but by slightly turning him over on his left side, these valve sounds can be faintly heard. He has some distress in the chest, and suffers from palpitation of the heart.

Trac. 19. (——)

These tracings were taken with the patient lying on his back. Pressure of the upper 2 oz., and of the lower 3 oz. A pressure of 6 oz. cuts off all movement of the lever.

There was marked oedema, and urine scant. The patient was considered in great danger of "*shiyoshin*," and was put on drastic cathartics, strong diuretics, large doses of digitalis with small doses of strychnia.

Six days later the next tracing was taken. No special change noticeable in the patient's condition, though he says he feels more comfortable.

Trac. 20. (——)

This tracing was taken in the same way the first series was. Pulse, 98. Pressure, 3 oz. In this tracing there are increasing premonitions of a tidal wave. The ventricular systole is less forcible, but the indications of the tracing are not more hopeful than at the first.

Seven days later the next series of tracings were taken. They show no improvement. The patient is gradually losing ground. The hands and feet are cold and slightly purple. They look and feel much as the extremities of a person in collapse from cholera, except that the cuticle still retains its elasticity. The voice has grown very weak, and the patient is suffering from marked dyspnoea. The diaphragm is partially paralyzed, and respiration is largely carried on by the respiratory muscles of the chest.

Trac. 21. (——)

It is remarkable how long this patient holds out in eminent danger. But the following night slight "*shiyoshin*" developed, and the patient died 30 hours after the tracing was taken.

Partial loss of voice from the action of the *materies morbi* of kakké upon the recurrent laryngial nerves is frequently met with. Complete loss of voice from the same cause is occasionally seen. I was once called in consultation where complete loss of voice was among the first prominent symptoms of kakké. A few days later marked paralysis of the upper and lower extremities developed. Partial paralysis of the diaphragm from the action of kakké *materies morbi* upon the phrenic nerves is also frequently met with. I have never met with complete paralysis of this muscle except in one case, seen in consultation. In this case there was marked oedema, slight paralysis of the extremities, the heart was but little impaired, "*shiyoshin*" had not yet developed; there was full stomach resonance on percussion as high as the upper border of the sixth rib, and was not depressed during inspiration, the epigastrium and hypochondria were depressed during inspiration while the chest dilated, the patient could not take a long breath, and could only utter a few syllables in a feeble voice till fully out of breath. His dyspnoea and the toiling efforts of the respiratory muscles of the chest were distressing to behold. He died within 24 hours from dyspnoea and exhaustion.

Case 17. O.—O M. Female, aet. 28.

This is a case of puerperal kakké. The patient is of strong constitution. There was slight anaesthesia and weakness of the legs a few days before confinement. On the fifth and sixth days after labor she was on her feet. After this she began to grow worse, and ten days after confinement she could neither walk nor stand. She has gradually grown worse, and to-day, the 27th since the birth of her child, she cannot move either the legs or the feet, but can slightly move the toes. She can imperfecty raise the arms, but the wrists drop, and she cannot raise them, neither can she fully extend the fingers. She can make no impression on the Dynamometer, and her hands are so weak that I feel no resistance in withdrawing my finger from her grasp. There is great oedema. Urine scant, about 450 cm. in 24 hours. Micturition difficult,— slow, laborious and tedious,—there is partial paralysis* of the muscular walls of the bladder.

Condition of blood, Table III.—No. 8.

---

* See Addenda,—Paralysis of Bladder.

Temp. 37.5° C. Pulse, 116. No sense of special weakness is indicated by the touch. If the arm is elevated, the force of the pulse is much diminished. The click of the aortic cusps is weaker than that of the pulmonary.

Trac. 22. (——)

The tracings were taken with the patient lying down. Pressure of the first tracing 1 oz., of the second 3 oz., and of the third 5 oz. A pressure of $6\frac{1}{2}$ oz. cut off all motion of the lever.

The friends were informed that "*shiyoshin*" was liable to occur at any time and the patient die. Three days after this tracing was taken, a slight paralysis of "*shiyoshin*" occurred, and the patient died within 24 hours.

Case 18. S.—S. *Male, aet.* 33.

The patient is of strong constitution. This is the third year in succession that this man has had kakké. He has now been ill 110 days. The symptoms were mild till within the last 20 days, since then he has gradually grown worse. For the last 15 days he has not been able to stand, and he cannot now even *suwari*. Some ten days ago his voice began to grow weak, and now he can only speak in a low whisper. He suffers from dyspnoea. He can only speak a few short syllables till he is compelled to take breath. There is partial paralysis of the vocal cords and diaphragm. He can neither flex nor extend the legs, he can partially flex and extend the feet and move the toes. He can raise his arms. Dynm. R. H. 21, L. H. 22.

Condition of blood, Table III.—No. 77.

Resp. 36. Pulse, 126, and weak. If the arm is elevated the pulse is still more weakened. The click of the aortic and pulmonary cusps is but faintly heard, nor can I distinguish between them. The first sound of the heart is flattened. The respiration is irregular, a few rapid inspirations, then a long rest, followed by a few slow and prolonged inspirations. The respiratory muscles of the chest toil in the respiratory effort.

Trac. 23. (——)

The friends of the patient were informed that "*shiyoshin*" was liable to occur at any time and the patient die. Some three hours after this tracing was taken a severe paroxysm of "*shiyoshin*" came on and lasted about two hours, when the patient died.

The tracings under this head all partake of the same general character. Dicrotism is strongly marked, the heart is suffering from partial muscular paralysis, accompanied by *vaso-motor* debility.

6.—During "Shiyoshin."

Case 19. Y.—C. *Male, aet.* 19.

The patient is of strong constitution. This was a mild case, and had been ill some 30 days. He was attending the hospital as an out patient, continued his work and did not appear much discommoded by his slight muscular paralysis. He had not reported himself for some ten days. He said he had been gradually growing worse for the last three days. Last night he was taken with pain in the bowels and distress in the chest. This gradually grew worse, and this morning he had several very copious movements of the bowels. He became faint and slight "*shiyoshin*" developed, when I was sent for. The paroxysm of "*shiyoshin*" had passed off before I reached the patient. The pulse was weak, there was marked pallor, the extremities were cold, and the patient was in a state of partial collapse. The tracings were at once taken.

Trac. 24. (——)

The tracings were taken with the patient lying on his back. Pressure of the upper tracing $2\frac{1}{2}$ oz., of the second 3 oz., and of the lower 4 oz. A doctor near by who was called in, said that no pulse could be felt at the wrist during "*shiyoshin*," and that it had only become perceptible just before I reached the patient. The tracing shows the heart in a weak condition, full dicrotism and very low tension.

Cases are frequently met with where the first prominent symptoms of kakké developed just as this did, with diarrhoea and distress in the chest. Such cases of "*shiyoshin*" are occasionally met, but diarrhoea does not generally accompany kakké; obstinate constipation is much more frequently met with.

Condition of blood, Table III.—No. 84. A large number of kakké micro-organism were found in this patient's blood.

There was some oedema. The patient was at once given digitalis, strichnia and whiskey, and put upon an active course of cathartics and diuretics.

The patient at once began to improve, and six days later the following tracings were taken.

Trac. 25. (——)

These tracings show quite an improvement over those taken immediately after the paroxysm of "*shiyoshin*." The tension though weak has much improved, and the *vaso-motor* tone is better. The patient continued to improve and after a time recovered.

Case 20. *J.—S. Female, aet.* 19.

The patient is of strong constitution. She has been suffering from kakké for about 50 days. General anasarca is marked. There is general pallor with some pigmentation, giving that peculiar anaemic expression so common in kakké. She has grown rapidly worse during the last ten days, for the last five days she has not been able to walk, and for the last two days she has not been able to stand. She can scarcely *suwari* at present. She suffers much from dyspnoea, palpitation of the heart, and distress in the chest, all of which are much increased by the slightest effort to move. Dynm. R. H. 15, L. H. 15.

Condition of blood, Table III.—No. 13.

She cannot lie down on account of distressing dyspnoea, and as she lies propped up in a reclining position, with heaving chest and marked praecordial pulsation, she is a pitiable picture of extreme distress.

Temp. 38.9° C. Resp. 50. Pulse, 140.

There are some moist *rales* over the chest, the patient is troubled with cough and frothy expectoration. There is evidently some effusion into the bronchi; but no evidence of effusion into either the pleura or pericardium. The pulse is much weakened when the arm is raised. The click of the aortic or pulmonary cusps cannot be distinguished. The heart sounds are feebly heard, and that over the right side of the heart flat. Slight paroxysms of "*shiyoshin*" began yesterday, and have occurred every three or four hours since. At times they are much severer than usual. The patient has not been able to rest for the last two nights, and her strength is beginning to fail.

Trac. 26. (——)

These tracings were taken with the patient reclining, propped up in bed. Pressure, 1 oz. After the first tracing was taken, a slight paroxysm of "*shiyoshin*" came on. During this paroxysm, which lasted about half an hour, the pulse could only be distinguished faintly at times, but was not sufficiently strong to cause the lever to vibrate. As soon as the severity of the paroxysm had in a measure passed off so the pulse could be felt at the wrist, and the lever began to have slight vibration, the second tracing was taken. During this paroxysm the patient's distress was extreme and the extremities became purple. This tracing shows the pulse hyperdicrotic and irregular, with very weak *vaso-motor* power. These conditions are much more marked in the last tracing.

The case was considered hopeless, but the patient was at once put on powerful doses of digitalis, whiskey, and moderate doses of strychnia. The kidneys were cupped, and profuse catharsis and diuresis were promptly secured.

The next day the patient was much more comfortable. Symptoms of poison from digitalis were beginning to be manifest. The dose was accordingly diminished slightly, aconite added, and the dose of strychnia increased. Within a few days the patient began to improve, though the action of the heart continued quite irregular.

Twelve days later the next tracing was taken. The patient can now lie down with comfort, and can *suwari* with ease. Dynm. R. H. 20, L. H. 20.

Resp. 40. No cough. Pulse, 106, and feels much stronger to the touch. If the arm is elevated the pulse is weakened. The click of the aortic cusps is very faint to-day, that of the pulmonary inaudible. The pulse is still weak and irregular, gradually changing from fast to slow, to be followed by a few rapid beats. Yesterday the pulse frequently remitted, to-day there is no remission.

Trac. 27. (——)

These tracings were taken with the patient *suwari-ing* in bed, with her arm resting on a low form. Pressure, 3 oz. The second tracing shows the action of the heart in its transition from the usual rate to one much slower. These tracings show a marked improvement over those first taken.

Trac. 28. (——)

This tracing shows the action of the heart 15 days later. Pressure 1 oz. The patient feels quite comfortable, but becomes dizzy if she rises up and attempts to walk.

Trac. 29. (——)

This tracing shows the action of the heart 48 days later, or 75 days after the paroxysms of "*shiyoshin*." Pressure 1 oz. The patient said she felt perfectly well, but the action of the heart is not quite normal yet.

SHIYOSHIN *is thus seen to consist in a paroxysm of increased depression of the nervous energies controling the circulation and respiration;—a more or less marked collapse of the paralyzed cardiac muscles and the paralyzed* VASO-MOTOR *system.* A complete collapse and death may and often does occur in the first of these paroxysms, but most generally they occur at shorter and shorter intervals, becoming more and more severe, while the nervous energies of the circulation and respiration gather up less and less during the intervals, till complete prostration and collapse occur.

7.—AFFECTED NERVOUS CENTERS.

Case 21. I.—K. Male, aet. 53.

The patient is of strong constitution and has now been ill about 150 days. He is pale and appears anaemic. He walks with difficulty, can squat down but cannot rise up, and stands on tip-toe with difficulty. Dynm. R.H. 80, L.H. 75. Condition of blood, Table III., No. 4. He suffers from palpitation of the heart and distress in the chest, and is made much worse by slight exercise. Pulse 104, feels strong, but with something of a "water-hammer" impulse, and is weakened if the arm is elevated. The click of the aortic cusps is weaker than that of the pulmonary. There is praecordial pulsation and the heart toils in its action. While quiet he says he suffers no special inconvenience.

Trac. 30. (———)

This tracing was taken with the patient sitting by a table. Three days later the next series of tracings was taken. In the mean time the patient had grown worse, though the pulse was reduced under strong doses of digitalis, the circulation was more disturbed by slight exercise, and the heart showed greater irritability and toiled more in its action. The patient was affected with stupor and the mind clouded. He not only failed to fully understand what was said to him, but his answers and talk were irrational and wandering.

Trac. 31. (———)

These tracings were taken with the patient lying down. Pressure of the first and second tracings 2 oz. and of the last 4 oz. After taking the first tracing the patient walked across the room and back, steadying himself by placing his hand on my shoulder, some little time was lost in adjusting the instrument, when the second tracing was taken. The instrument was then held in place on his arm while he walked across the room as before, and at once on lying down the last tracing was taken.

The action of the heart is seen to be more irregular than when the first tracing was taken, the pulse is very irregular, the respiratory curves marked but irregular, while slight exertion throws the heart into toilsome, frustrated action. This tracing suggests myocarditis.

Seven days later the next tracing was taken. In the mean time the patient had been kept perfectly quiet, and had been taking large doses of digitalis and small doses of strychnia. The action of the heart had improved, but the general paralysis had advanced. The patient's mind had also cleared up considerably.

Trac. 32. (———)

These tracings were taken with the patient lying down. Pressure, $1\frac{1}{2}$ oz. After the first tracing was taken, the patient was assisted to walk across the room and back, and after the lapse of a few minutes the second tracing was taken. Then the instrument was held in place on the arm while the patient was assisted across the room and back, and at once on resuming the recumbent position the third tracing was taken.

These tracings show a marked improvement in the condition of the heart. After a time the muscular paralysis began to improve, and the patient made a complete recovery, without showing any nervous complications other than those connected with kakké. The mind of kakké patients generally remains clear to the last; occasionally the intellect becomes clouded, but seldom so much as in this case.

I have assigned the phenomena presented in the tracings of this case, especially that of trac. 31, to the action of the kakké *materies morbi* upon the cardiac and respiratory nervous centers. The tracings in this case are peculiar and not often met with in kakké; they differ materially in character from those assigned to cardiac paralysis from the influence of the *materies morbi* upon the peripheral nerves of circulation and respiration. The cerebral disturbance together with other symptoms led me to this conclusion. The marked improvement in the action of the heart in a comparatively short time goes to exclude myocarditis. But from the peculiar muscular hyperasthesia of the extremities in some cases, I am disposed to think that there may occasionally be a form of myositis, and analogy would lead us to conclude that there might also be a form of myocarditis in kakké.

8.—Simulates Heart Disease.

Case 22. O.—T. Male, aet. 24.

The patient is of strong constitution. He had a light attack of kakké last year; this year he says he escaped, but since early in September (now about four months) he has been much annoyed with unpleasant heart symptoms. He says he is perfectly well and strong, but that he is troubled with palpitation of the heart after walking a short distance, with slight distress in the chest. He has visited different medical men throughout the country, but has only been flustered by their opinions and treatment. I found no symptoms of heart disease, but slight symptoms of kakké.
Condition of blood, Table III.—No. 16.

Trac. 33. (———)

The tracing was taken to see whether the sphygmograph would show any signs of heart weakness, and was taken with the patient sitting by a table. Pressure, 5 oz. The patient refused to run a short distance, that I might see the action of the heart under the influence of exercise. He was treated for kakké, and his heart symptoms soon passed off.

Anomalous cases of heart disease are frequently met with in Japan; they are generally considered functional, or perhaps neurotic. I find many such cases associated with slight symptoms of kakké, and the probability of their being such should always be taken into consideration. The proper use of the microscope and cultures will enable the physician to definitely decide in regard to this point.

9.—Tracings of Marey's and Pond's Sphygmograph in Kakké, contrasted.

Case 23. K. Male, aet. 15.

Of strong constitution. Has been ill 35 days, complains of palpitation of the heart and distress in the chest on slight exercise.

Trac. 34. (———)

Tracings 1 and 2 were taken with Marey's instrument, 1 before exercise, and 2 after. Tracings 3 and 4 were taken with Pond's instrument, 3 before exercise, and 4 after. The tracings were taken the same day, and under the same circumstance, first with one instrument and then the other, excepting after exercise; when each one was taken immediately after the same amount of exercise.

Case 24. H.—K. Male, aet. 20.

Of strong constitution, has been ill 45 days.

Trac. 35. (———)

Tracings 1 and 2 were taken with Marey's instrument, 1 before exercise, and 2 after. Tracings 3 and 4 were taken with Pond's instrument, 3 before exercise, and 4 after. The tracings were taken as those of trac. 34 were, under essentially the same circumstances.

Case 25. H. Male, aet. 19.

Of strong constitution, has been ill 40 days.

Trac. 36. (———)

These tracings were taken as those of 34 and 35 were, and under essentially the same circumstances. Tracings 1 and 2 were taken with Marey's instrument, 1 before exercise, and 2 after. Tracings 3 and 4 were taken with Pond's instrument, 3 before exercise, and 4 after.

10.—Pond's Instrument used as a Cardiograph.

Case 26. N.—H. Male, aet. 16.

Of average constitution, has been ill 38 days. Heart sounds normal. Is comfortable while still; cannot walk any distance from distress in the chest and dyspnoea produced by exercise. These tracings were taken with the patient seated, and by placing the foot of the instrument over the point of most forcible apex percussion.

Trac. 37. (———)

Case 27. N. Male, aet. 14.

Of strong constitution. Has been ill 20 days. Anaesthesia and muscular paralysis very slight. Suffers from palpitation of the heart and distress in the chest.

Trac. 38. (———)

The upper tracing was taken before exercise, the lower after.

Case 28. K.—H. Male, aet. 21.

Of strong constitution. Has been ill 40 days. The upper extremities are not affected; the lower but slightly. Complains chiefly of inability to walk from the thumping in his chest. The heart acts vigorously; pulse, 118.

Trac. 39. (———)

The upper tracing was taken before exercise, the lower after.

SUMMARY.

There was no organic disease of either the heart or arteries in any of the cases here presented, and no functional derangement of the heart other than that produced by kakké.

1.—*A Kakké Tracing.* It will be observed by looking over these tracings that they are marked by certain prevailing characteristics, viz: (*a*) The very sudden and high upstroke of the ventricular systole. (*b*) The precipitous descent from the apex of the percussion wave. (*c*) Dicrotism. These points are so characteristic of the vascular and respiratory derangement in kakké as to constitute what may very properly be termed a *kakké tracing.*

2.—*The first deviation of the circulatory system in kakké from the normal, is one of cardiac excitement.* In the early stages of kakké and in mild cases, the sudden and tall upstroke of the percussion wave points to a condition of *cardiac excitement.**

3.—Diminished VASO-MOTOR *tension.* The low condition of arterial tension is due to loss of *vaso-motor* tone, producing a relaxed condition of the arterial and capillary system, and permitting a free out-flow from the arteries. This also is the chief cause of the precipitous descent from the apex of the percussion wave. This interpretation is in accordance with the teachings of clinical experience. The sensation imparted by the pulse to the finger on the artery is that the blood courses along the artery in distinct waves to be completely emptied in the interval. Also the sense of coldness of the extremities which the patient experiences as the case advances, and the purple hue of the fingers and toes, denotes a loss of *vaso-motor* tone with a relaxed condition of the capillary system and diminished cardiac power. The advance of the purple hue up the extremities during *shiyoshin* (and also frequently previous to and denoting the approach of *shiyoshin*), points also to continued loss of *vaso-motor* tone, with increased relaxation of the vascular system and accumulation of blood in the capillaries.

4.—*The elements of danger in kakké are found in the impaired condition of the heart and circulation.* It will be noticed that the relation which exists between the condition of the vascular system and the general condition of the patient is subject to great variation. (*a*) The tracings in some cases show very irregular action of the heart, an abnormal high and sudden upstroke of the ventricular systole with loss of arterial tension, when the general symptoms were not those of grave danger. This is a very common condition; and cases are frequently met with where this contrast is so great that the patient is considered suffering from serious functional derangement or neurosis of the heart, while the ordinary symptoms of kakké are so slight as to be passed by unnoticed. (*b*) Again when the general symptoms were grave the tracings often show but slight deviation from the normal. (*c*) However grave the general symptoms may be, so long as the condition of the circulation and respiration remain good, there is no occasion for alarm. But however mild the general symptoms may be, if the condition of the circulation is much impaired, the indications are those of grave danger. The physician must look to the condition of the heart and circulation in kakké to determine the elements of danger in the case.

5.—*The extent to which the heart and* VASO-MOTOR *system are affected in kakké, is relatively subject to considerable change.* The transversly striated muscular fibers of the heart with its complex nervous supply endow it with an automatic *motor* power, while the rest of the circulatory system is endowed only with a *vaso-motor* power. Either of these forces may be separately impaired, or the heart and arterially system may be similarly, though not necessarily equally, enfeebled. The sphygmograph enables us to tell which of, and to what extent, these powers are affected. The general muscular system, especially the muscles of the extremities, suffer paralysis and atrophy from the affected cerebro-spinal nerves. The heart being a muscular organ is liable to and does suffer in the same way. The relaxed condition of the arterial and capillary system shows that the *vaso-motor* nerves of the sympathetic system are affected. (*a*) In some cases the sudden and tall upstroke of the percussion wave shows that the muscular grasp of the heart upon the contained blood is strong, giving a vigorous ventricular systole; while in the same tracing there is a precipitous fall from the apex of the percussion wave, a fully dicrotic or hyperdicrotic pulse with greatly reduced arterial tension, denoting a marked loss of *vaso-motor* tone. (*b*) Again in other cases with weak cardiac action there is a measure of arterial tension. (*c*) My experience with the sphygmograph in kakké has taught

---

* The first complaint that kakké patients make along with that of anaesthsia and oedema of the legs is (*ikidoshii*) of cardiac dyspnoea.

me that loss of *vaso-motor* tone is fraught with graver danger than loss of cardiac muscular power.

6.—*The condition preceding* SHIYOSHIN. When there is marked dicrotism, loss of *vaso-motor* tone, and a relaxed arterial and capillary system with free outflow, even though the sudden and high upstroke of the percussion wave show favorable cardiac power, yet *shiyoshin* is liable to occur at any time.

7.—SHIYOSHIN. In the above condition the toiling heart may at any time become exhausted, the powers of circulation suffer a partial collapse, and the phenomena of *shiyoshin* be developed.

8.—*These various states of the circulation are consistent with one pathological condition.* All these variable conditions of the cardiac and vascular phenomena can be explained by the action of the *materias morbi* of kakké upon different portions of the cerebro-spinal nerves and sympathetic system.

ADDENDA.

Kakké presents some peculiar features of interest for study and investigation, among which we may mention

AGE.—Age as a predisposing cause to kakké is readily admitted by those who have had some experience with this disease. The most susceptible age is from 16 to 28 or 32. A very large ratio of those seen in general practice will be young men between the ages of 17 and 25. I have never met with a case under 12 years of age, and from extensive inquiry, have not heard of a case under 11. Children appear to enjoy an absolute immunity from kakké.—I have never met with a case over 63 years of age, and am informed that it very seldom occurs over 60 and never over 65. Why there should be an absolute immunity from kakké till approaching adolescence, an intensified susceptibility to its influence during early manhood, and again a greatly reduced susceptibility if not immunity from this disease in old age, is a phenomenon worthy of consideration and investigation.

RECURRENCE.—One attack of kakké appears to render the patient more liable to subsequent attacks. A large number of those seen will state that they have suffered repeatedly from kakké in successive years. Many have had from three to five, seven and ten attacks in as many successive years. Occasionally you will meet those who have repeatedly suffered from kakké, yet have one or two years remission. Last year I met with two persons each of whom had suffered from kakké for the last twenty successive years.

SEX.—Women are much less likely to be affected with kakké than men. A common estimate among the Japanese for the number of cases of kakké occurring among women is 4-6 per cent. But this estimate is much too low. While women do enjoy a peculiar immunity from this disease, the difference between the number of women and men affected is not so great as would at first appear. Women generally have the disease much milder than men; and many of them affected with kakké have it so light that they do not apply for medical aid. Of the number of cases recorded in my case-book, over 16 per cent. have been women; and an estimate of from 10 to 15 per cent. would be a close approach to the ratio of female cases occurring in kakké.

PUERPERAL KAKKÉ.—Though women in general enjoy a marked immunity from kakké, yet in the puerperal state they are quite subject to this disease, and when taken in this condition it is attended with a marked fatality. Of the female kakké cases coming under my observation over 36 per cent. have been puerperal. Kakké may occur during lactation, in such cases it is not attended by special fatality; but it is very liable to occur shortly before or after child-birth, and in such cases it is most likely to be severe and attended with a high rate of mortality. Of such cases falling under my observation, over 65 per cent. have been fatal. When an *enceinte* woman is taken with kakké, she should at once be removed to a locality exempt from this disease.

URINE.—It is but seldom that traces of albumen are found in the urine of kakké patients. Of the cases coming under my observation, the urine of three or four contained for a short time a small quantity of albumen, that showed no traces of it after recovery. In almost all kakké cases the urinary secretion is diminished, and if the case is severe very markedly diminished. It frequently runs down to 900, 600, 300 cubic centimeters in 24 hours, and occasionally as low as 200 or 150 c.c. In some cases under my observation it has run down as low as 100-50 c.c. in 24 hours for several successive days, yet no oedema occurred. But such cases are most likely to die. The importance of keeping up the secretion of urine to the fullest extent should never be lost sight of in treating cases of kakké. If the circulation is not specially affected and the secretion of urine can be kept up to a reasonable quantity of 900 or 750 c.c. per day, the case may be considered hopeful. But if this secretion runs down below 600 or 500 c.c. in 24 hours and cannot be brought up, the case should be considered doubtful; for though the condition of the circulation be good, with so small a secretion of urine the powers of circulation will soon show signs of failure. The secretion of urine frequently ceases some hours before death.

PARALYSIS OF THE BLADDER.—Partial paralysis of the muscular walls of the bladder are occasionally met with in cases of kakké, so that micturition becomes tedious and imperfect. But if the case progresses favorably this will pass off after some days. A few cases of complete paralysis of the bladder, a short time before death, have also come under my observation; when, although the patient had not urinated for some time, yet a reasonable amount was drawn off with a catheter.

EXPLANATION OF TRACINGS.

Plate I.—This is simply introduced for convenience of comparison. The upper tracing is taken from Dr. A. E. Sansom's "*Physical Diagnosis of the Heart.*"

"The normal pulse-trace magnified: *a b*, percussion up stroke; *a b c*, percussion wave; *c d e*, tidal wave; *d e f*, dicrotic wave; at *e*, aortic notch; *f a*, dicrotic period."

The lower tracings :—

1.—"Normal adult trace."—Dr. Pond. The tension, however, is too low in this trace.

2.—"*Sphygmographic tracing of Normal Pulse.*"—Dr. Byrom Bramwell. The tension in this trace is good.

3.—"*Mahomed's Method of guaging high tension.*"—Bramwell.

Plates II.-IX. inclusive.—Tracings of "kakké" cases.

Tracings from 1 to 6 inclusive.—Slight cardiac debility; Cases 1 to 5 inclusive.

Trace 7.—Irregular action of the heart; Case 6. Also tracings 13, 27, 37, 38 and 39 present irregular action of the heart.

Tracings from 8 to 10 inclusive.—Effects of varying pressure; Cases 7 to 9 inclusive.

Tracings from 11 to 14 inclusive.—Effects of exercise; Cases 10 to 12 inclusive.

Tracings from 15 to 23 inclusive.—Weakness predicting "*shiyoshin*"; Cases 13 to 18 inclusive.

Tracings 24 and 26.—During "*shiyoshin*"; Cases 19 and 20.

Tracings 25, 27, 28 and 29.—Recovery after "*shiyoshin*"; Cases 19 and 20.

Tracings 30 to 32 inclusive.—Affected cerebrospinal centers; Case 21.

Trace 33; Case 22.—A case simulating heart disease.

Tracings 34 to 36 inclusive.—Marey's and Pond's Sphygmographs in kakké, contrasted; Cases 23 to 25.

Tracings 37 to 39 inclusive.—Cardiac tracings with Pond's instrument; Cases 26 to 28.

Printed by Libri Plureos GmbH in Hamburg, Germany